THE RISE OF SILAS LAPHAM

NOTES

including

- *Howells — His Life and Works*
- *Introduction to the Novel*
- *Summary of the Plot*
- *List of Characters*
- *Summaries and Commentaries*
- *Analytical Commentary*
- *Questions and Answers for Review*
- *Theme Topics*
- *Bibliography*

by
Pat Keating

Cliffs Notes

INCORPORATED

LINCOLN, NEBRASKA 68501

Editor

Gary Carey, M.A.
University of Colorado

Consulting Editor

James L. Roberts, Ph.D.
Department of English
University of Nebraska

ISBN 0-8220-1147-6
© Copyright 1964
by
Cliffs Notes, Inc.
All Rights Reserved
Printed in U.S.A.

1995 Printing

Cliffs Notes, Inc.   Lincoln, Nebraska

CONTENTS

WILLIAM DEAN HOWELLS
1837-1920

HIS LIFE AND WORKS

Born in Martin's Ferry, Ohio, William Dean Howells rose from the lowest position on his father's newspaper staff to novelist, critic, and spokesman for realism. From his father, he acquired equalitarian ideas; from his reading of Swedenborg, he gained a persisting ethical bent. He incorporated these elements into the poetry that he wrote late at night after he had finished his work on the newspaper. He read Cervantes, Heine, and Shakespeare and learned Spanish, German, and French.

He did not fully put his talents to work until after he wrote the campaign biography of Lincoln. Money earned from this biography afforded him a trip to New England, where he met James Russell Lowell. Lowell used his influence to help Howells gain the United States consul post in Venice.

Following his assignment, he returned to the United States to edit and popularize *The Atlantic Monthly*. He published works of Mark Twain and Henry James in an effort to make the magazine nationally known.

He wrote travel novels. The most important were *A Chance Acquaintance* (1873), *A Foregone Conclusion* (1875), *The Lady of Aroostook* (1875), *Their Wedding Journey* (1881), *Indian Summer* (1886).

As a spokesman for realism, he wrote an essay entitled "Henry James Jr.," which asserted that "the art of Fiction has become a finer art in our day than it was with Dickens and Thackery." His realistic novels included *The Rise of Silas Lapham* (1885), *A Hazard of New Fortune* (1889), *Annie Kilburn* (1891), *A Traveller from Altruria* (1894).

The quality of Howells' work may be questioned today, for even he recognized that he was fading from literary acclaim in his later years. *The Rise of Silas Lapham* is not only the most popular of his novels, but it is probably the one best in literary quality, because it is so representative of the early realistic novel.

He wrote 34 other novels, 29 plays, 9 books of travel, 6 books of literary criticism, 4 books of poetry, and 25 miscellaneous works.

INTRODUCTION AND PLOT SUMMARY

When reading and studying *The Rise of Silas Lapham*, recognition of the existence of a plot and subplot is necessary. Knowledge of how they relate to each other is also important. In the William Dean Howells novel, a business story dominates a secondary love triangle. Silas Lapham earns a fortune in the paint business through opportunism, greed, and driving ambition. He wants his daughter to marry into the aristocratic Corey family to gain the social prominence the backwoods Laphams have never attained. Silas' conduct in managing his business and Irene's love affair are based on the same materialistic set of values which draw the two stories together.

Silas' rise to fortune and the contrived love affair of Irene are romantic aspects of the novel which are only temporary and end tragically. Silas loses his business because he loans too much money to a former partner to redeem his soul from the sin of greed; he had used his partner's money to make the business profitable and then forced the partner out of the enterprise. Irene's love affair is tragically ended when her supposed lover, Tom Corey, reveals that he loves her sister instead.

Silas' moral rise after his tragic downfall and Irene's similar realistic development after her love affair are somewhat parallel. Silas will not save his business by continuing to extort money from unknowing parties; he now thinks of others rather than himself. His daughter also compensates for her lost lover by helping and thinking of her father at the time of his financial crisis.

Being realistic, the novel presents characters who have both tragic and comic qualities and fates. Together these stories reveal some of Howells' comments on society and art. All of these aspects — tragicomedy, romanticism, realism, morality, society, and art, plus Americanism and universality, will be investigated in relationship to the plot and characters.

CHARACTERS

THE LAPHAM FAMILY

Silas

This central character is presented as a tragic as well as a comic hero. Because of his greed and pride, he loses his business, constituting a tragic downfall; but his moral decision to live for others raises him spiritually, bringing him to a happy, peaceful state of mind in the end. As a tragic hero, he must be presented as being a better than average man. His great wealth places him out of the ordinary realm of men. Additionally, he must have a tragic flaw; Silas fulfills this by having a desire for wealth above all considerations and by having an exalted pride in his wealth. As a comic character, he must display some quirks that are not moral flaws or characteristics that are not damning. Silas likes to brag, for instance, about his family, his paint, and his new home. He, also, has false social aspirations, as illustrated by his building a new home which he thinks will put him on the same social level with the Coreys.

As a tragic comic hero, Silas finds in his middle age that he cannot attain his romantic but impossible social aspiration. His comic traits do not make him a comical butt, and his tragic downfall does not make him an actual hero; but, instead, he is a man much like ourselves. The psychology of his makeup is presented realistically, and in the end, he is "sadder but wiser," chastened but not totally defeated.

He is romantic in regard to the wealth that has made his life dreamlike and immediately makes the mistake of matching his beautiful, instead of his intelligent daughter, with Tom Corey. His realism grows as the novel progresses, for he later faces the reality of his moral fault of taking advantage of Rogers, the reality of his social position as a crude, uneducated backwoodsman, and the real necessity for Penelope to marry Corey.

Silas has few aesthetic values, for he covers the New England landscape with advertisements for his paint. His plans for a home are ugly, and he has no appreciation for art, as shown by his saying that the quality of a painting depends solely upon the price paid.

Like the people on the boat that he takes to his summer home, he is a commonplace man with nothing but the American poetry of vivid purpose to light him up. Uncultured, he prefers newspapers, theater, and lectures to books. He does not like to see tragedy on the stage because there is enough of it in real life. The Coreys he finds to be offensively aristocratic, and he does not consider associating with them until he needs to introduce his daughters to society. Because of his great wealth, he takes a condescending attitude toward them, not realizing his money is all he has. His money, he believes, makes him equal if not better.

A hard worker, his wife says he slaves harder every year. Of course, this is the only way he knows to make more money. Walker, his bookkeeper, says that Silas knows what he wants and goes after it. Even though a stubborn, natural-born businessman, he does have trouble working out complicated arithmetical problems. Sharing management with Rogers or anyone else is more than he can endure. Standing alone, he believes every man should be able to take care of himself rather than to be taken care of like a woman. Although not brilliant, he is intelligent, shrewd, and sensible.

His relationship with his wife has degenerated from one of sharing to secrecy about his business. Yet, they like to talk to each other in a blunt way: "it is the New England way of expressing perfect confidence and tenderness." Whenever anything goes wrong, Mrs. Lapham can still expect this broad-shouldered, square-chinned man to tell her.

Persis
Silas' wife was a schoolteacher and represented a social step up for him when he married her before his wealthier days. She

worked well with him, helping him with the paint business until they were so wealthy that she only needed to find ways to spend their fortune. Silas says, "If it hadn't been for her, the paint wouldn't have come to anything. I used to tell her it wa'n't the seventy-five per cent of purr-ox-eyed of iron in the *ore* that made that paint go; it was the seventy-five per cent of purr-ox-eyed of iron in *her*."

Mrs. Lapham is a Puritan for whom the fire of guilt for sin and spiritual interference in the course of man's activities has nearly burnt out. She tells Silas that she does not believe in the Lord interfering a great deal, but when he makes Rogers a loan she feels He's interfered this time. Her lukewarm Puritanism extends to her lack of ability to help Silas make a moral decision concerning the English settlers. She would almost rather see him sell the mills and remain wealthy, repenting the rest of his life.

She is not a tragic or comic figure, but a pathetic one, for her morality represents the dry rot of the Puritan culture that will eventually crumble and disappear. As Silas' conscience, she is unsparing, caustic, pessimistic, temperamental, conservative, rigid, vindictive, and most of all, petty.

Like other romantic women, she cannot help Silas cope with his problems and loses all sight of the issues at the crisis. When Silas must decide upon either selling to the English agents at an unfair price or losing his business, her tears are the only help she can give him. She remains the weak, romantic figure throughout the novel. She believes that Tom Corey loves Irene and cannot cope with the situation when she finds that he does not. When the truth is known, she overemphasizes the emotional situation and must turn to Silas, who is more realistic at this point in the novel.

Persis Lapham, at least, recognizes her place in society when Silas does not. Because she knows that her family is not on the Coreys' social and educational level, she is somewhat against associating with them. She objects to moving into the house on Back Bay and is happy to return to the farm.

Like Silas, she is not artistic and has poor taste in clothes, pictures, and travel. She is a representative of those American women who are not strong enough to aid their husbands in the greatest hours.

Penelope

The older daughter of Silas and Persis has a sense of humor which is not literary, coming in flashes and ripples, but rather droll and commonplace. She is plain but not practical like Irene. Instead, as her mother points out, she is a dreamer with twice as many brains as Irene. Her character is set at the beginning of the novel and does not change even after her love affair with Tom Corey.

Penelope represents the witty but plain romantic woman. Like the heroines in popular contemporary novels, she is confronted with the problem of having the man believed to love her sister really in love with her. Also, like these heroines, she attempts to give up the lover in a passionate outburst of self-sacrifice. Reality and the pressure of her realistic father and Tom Corey help force her to marry him, but it is more her romantic burst of passion for him that makes her say, "Yes."

The marriage does not immediately advance her position in society, for she and Tom go to Mexico to live and work after their marriage. One of Tom's sisters says, "As she's quite unformed, socially, there is a chance that she will form herself on the Spanish manner, if she stays there long enough, and that when she comes back she will have the charm of, not olives, perhaps, but *tortillas,* whatever they are: something strange and foreign, even if it's borrowed."

Irene

Irene, the younger daughter of the Laphams, has an "innocence which is almost vegetable," Howells points out. Her mother and older sister understand that Irene's eyes always express a great deal more than Irene ever thinks or feels. The Corey women, however, find Irene to be very pretty and well-behaved but very insipid. Tom Corey says, "She is interesting by her own limitations." And, Mrs. Lapham admits that she is not equal to Tom intellectually. "I'd ten times rather she was going to marry such a fellow as *you* were Si, that had to make every inch of his own way, and she had to help him. It's in her."

Irene is the ideal romantic girl—beautiful, unintelligent, and passive. She is like a flower—close to nature and unlearned. Although she becomes stronger after her love affair with Tom Corey is abruptly ended, she is not further developed. Practical enough to know that she must leave home after the blow, she does not return until the need for her arises during her father's difficulties with business. Her practical abilities are an asset to the family, as she keeps the house in perfect order. A better housekeeper than a student, she does not mentally fit into the Coreys' society, where but for her father's money, she might have been their maid.

THE COREYS

Bromfield

Silas Lapham finds Bromfield Corey to be offensively aristocratic. Silas disapproves of the fact that Bromfield has always let his father's wealth take care of him. He has traveled in Europe and studied painting. Mrs. Corey married him in Rome when he was a rich young painter who said so much better things than he painted. He continues to say charming things when they return to Boston. Actively but rather passively extravagant with his father's money, he is not adventurous with it. His tastes are simple, and he has no expensive habits. Secluded life suits him best, and the Coreys' life has been uneventful.

Bromfield is the spokesman for the intelligent, aristocratic class, although he says that to his relief he has found himself to be of common clay rather than porcelain. "If I get broken, I can be easily replaced," he says.

His uselessness is not an understatement, for he is not actively involved in any project that makes him valuable to the world. He does not paint, but rather theorizes about it. He has found that it is absurd for him to paint for pay, and ridiculous to paint for nothing; so, he does not paint at all.

As a representative of the aristocratic class, he seems alien to the American culture. Walker, Lapham's bookkeeper, mistakes Bromfield for an Italian correspondent when the painter visits Silas at the office. Bromfield realizes that this nearly foreign culture, which he represents, is a society that is dying because it has narrow conventions and lacks creativity. When Tom returns from Texas with new ideas, Bromfield knows that the creativity of one of his own family will help to unseat his secure position as a social leader.

Realistically, Bromfield realizes his own sterile elegance is in competition with the crude materialism of Silas Lapham. He maintains, however, that civilization does not come from the noble savages like Lapham but, instead, from the reading citizens. Nevertheless, Bromfield appreciates the best in Silas. Bromfield's generesity and imagination let Tom work and marry with the Laphams in order to throw the Corey "sterile elegance" back into the main stream of life.

Bromfield is a humorous character used by Howells for comic relief.[1] Bromfield says that when Silas told him about his paint "he poured mineral paint all over me, till I could have been safely warranted not to crack or scale in any climate." He is gracefully witty at the expense of those who take life seriously. He tells his wife that Persis' extremely embarrassed and excited reaction to Mrs. Corey's call was because "you made her feel so. I can imagine how terrible you must have been in the character of an accusing spirit." When Mrs. Corey proposes the necessity of a dinner for the Laphams, Bromfield replies, "Ah, you overdid the accusing-spirit business, and this is reparation."

Anna

Bromfield's wife objects to her son Tom's marrying below his class to the inartistic Laphams. Nevertheless, she submits to it because of her fatalistic view of life. She is continually trying to endure the situation and do her best.

Tom

Tom Corey, in a way, replaces the son Silas Lapham lost at birth. Silas takes him as a son-in-law and as an employee. After

[1]George N. Bennett, *William Dean Howells: The Development of the Novelist* (Norman, Oklahoma: University of Oklahoma Press, 1959), p. 155

Silas meets Tom, he says, "I tell you if I had that fellow in the business with me I would make a man of him." Silas places more importance on Tom being a man than a son-in-law when he says, "He ain't going to take hold at all, if he don't mean paint in the first place and Irene afterward."

Tom does mean paint first, for he is energetic and career-minded, telling his father that he needs more than marriage to occupy him. His mother and father both recognize that he is not witty but a sympathetic listener to his father's wit. He has a clear mind which brings practical results with charming lucidity. He is popular because he does not try to outshine others.

He is a realist, seeing that he needs more than beauty in a wife and that he must use his energies to create a society based on energy and intelligence. He combines Silas' aggressiveness with Bromfield's good breeding to form a more solid American citizen for society.

Lily
Lily Corey is a frail girl who, like many romantic women, lives off her family's wealth. Her character is not developed.

Nanny
The Corey's youngest child, Nanny has read a great many novels with a keen sense of their inaccuracy as representations of life and has seen a great deal of life with a sad regret for its difference from fiction. She retitles the romantic novel *Tears, Idle Tears,* "*Slop, Silly Slop,*" Although she would prefer to be romantic, Nanny is more realistic than her mother and sister. She sees the changes that might be possible in Penelope's social education during her stay in Mexico. "At that distance we can correspond," she says, knowing they could not communicate if they were closer.

OTHER PEOPLE WHO AFFECT SILAS LAPHAM'S LIFE

Rogers
Silas forced Rogers out the paint business after he had made a start with his partner's capital. A tallish, thin man with a dust-colored

face and a dead, clerical air, which somehow suggested at once feebleness and tenacity, Rogers reappears to ask Silas for a loan. To protect the loan, Silas invests more money but is forced to demand repayment when his business has to compete with one that is underselling him. Rogers' proposed solution is for Silas to sell the mills that he holds as collateral to English agents at a price that is more than they are worth. He is Lapham's antagonist, as he places temptation before him. He causes Silas' moral rise as a comic character and his tragic fall as a businessman.

Sewell

Being a minister, Sewell is the counselor to whom Lapham turns for help when Penelope refuses to marry Tom Corey. Sewell, a realist, points out to Mrs. Lapham that Silas is right; Penelope is acting like a ruinous heroine in a romantic novel, and she is not helping Irene by refusing to marry Tom. Her self-sacrifice is ridiculous.

Sewell might be considered as a spokesman for Howells. His opinions on the purpose of the realistic novel are similar to those of the novelist.

Zerrilla Millon Dewey

Zerrilla Dewey is Silas' typist. He has hired her to help her and her mother, for they are the wife and daughter of Jim Millon, the man who took the bullet aimed at Lapham during the Civil War. Walker, Silas' head bookkeeper, suspects that she is Lapham's mistress.

Seymour

Mr. Seymour is Lapham's architect. He saves Silas from making a great deal of artistic blunders when building his house.

Bartley Hubbard

Hubbard writes a series called "Solid Men of Boston" for the *Boston Events* newspaper. His report on Silas Lapham is subtly biting, relating that Silas' parents taught their children the simple virtues of the Old Testament and Poor Richard's Almanac. In contrast with the Lapham's solid marriage, the Hubbards are near divorce. As far as the solidness of the marriages is concerned, the Laphams' Old Testament virtues have helped their marriage more than Hubbard's cynicism has strengthened his.

CHAPTER SUMMARIES AND COMMENTS

CHAPTER I

Summary

Bartley Hubbard has come to Silas Lapham's office to interview him for the "Solid Men of Boston" series in the *Boston Events* newspaper. Hubbard tells Silas, a nineteenth-century millionaire, that he wants his money or his life. "I guess you wouldn't want my life without the money," Lapham replies.

"Take 'em both," Bartley suggests.

Born on a northern Vermont farm near the Canadian border in 1820, Lapham was the son of poor and unpretentious, religious parents possessing sterling morality. Lapham, however, admired his mother more when she knelt before him at night washing his feet than when she knelt at prayer.

In 1835, his father discovered mineral paint on their farm in a pit left by an uprooted tree. Because of poverty, buildings were not being painted at that time. It was not until 1855, after his brothers had left the farm and Silas had returned from a three-month stay in Texas to operate a nearby tavern-stand, that he decided to mine and sell the paint. He married a schoolteacher, Persis, and together they built a fortune in paint that withstood sun and rain, not fading, chipping, or scaling.

Lapham shows his storeroom of paint, which is stocked in many sizes and colors. He shows Hubbard his first-rate paint, the Persis Brand. He continues to tell him of the advertisement for his paint on board fences, barns, and even large rocks, arguing that he does not understand why people object to this altering of the landscape. "I say the landscape was made for the man, and not the man for the landscape."

Lapham tells Hubbard that he did not have any influence in the government during the Civil War so he could not speculate by selling his paint for war supplies. Instead, at the insistence of his wife, he fought and returned a colonel. When he returned, he rushed the paint during the postwar boom with the help of a partner, who had the capital to back him. "He didn't know anything about paint," Lapham says. Silas bought his partner out in two years.

Leaving Lapham's office, Hubbard notices his attractive typist. "What an uncommonly pretty girl!" Hubbard comments.

"She does her work," Lapham replies.

Hubbard is given a ride back to the *Events* office in Lapham's buggy and learns of Silas' love for a fast horse. Writing a subtly cutting account of Lapham, Hubbard uses a tone that Silas will never detect.

Commentary

The length of the first chapter is significant because the great number of events, facts, and concepts that it contains prepare the reader for most of what is to follow. The Hubbard interview is the most objective, yet clever, way to present Silas' background. Howells has discovered a workable technique by which a great deal of data can be presented without being heavy like Balzac's narration. Hubbard's humor lightens the interview, and again this is a credit to Howells' style of writing.

Lapham's money is immediately stressed as his sole claim to fame. This is important later when the Coreys are presented with not only money but also education and social elegance as reasons for their prominence.

The sterling morality of Lapham's parents is pointed out, for it is significant that Silas Lapham, greedy capitalist, has come from moral origins. Later he can return to these origins when he refuses to cheat the English settlers in a business deal.

The fact that he admires his mother's working instead of praying points out Silas' philosophy of "Work and it shall be opened to you. Toil and you shall receive." He has discovered that he is much surer to get the things he wants by working for them, rather than by waiting for God to interfere in the course of daily events and give them to him.

His return from Texas to begin the mining and selling of paint is later paralleled by Tom Corey's return from the same state to work in the business with Silas.

Silas' defense of man using the landscape is a prediction of the artistic blunders he will make when planning the house he builds. It also forecasts why the artist Bromfield Corey is repelled by Lapham, who covers nature with a coat of paint.

The material downfall of Lapham is prepared for by the mention of the partner Lapham used for his capital. Howells later reveals that Mrs. Lapham plagues Silas with remembrance of his sin, and he seizes the opportunity to repay his partner by lending him money that he cannot return. The rise of an underselling paint company and a loss in the stock market force Lapham to demand repayment. His old partner proposes the unethical selling of the mills he has put up for collateral to English settlers. Lapham refuses and loses his business, but his concern for the good of the settlers redeems him morally.

Lapham's display of his stock also predicts his downfall, which is additionally due to his overstocking the market. Only the Persis Brand that he shows to Hubbard saves him as a businessman; the underselling paint company cannot produce such high quality, and Silas is able to maintain his family on his profits from it.

Hubbard's notice of Lapham's typist is significant, because she is later revealed to be Jim Millon's daughter. Millon is the man who took a bullet meant for Silas during the Civil War. Because his wife would object to his generosity, it is later revealed that he is secretly supporting the typist and her mother.

The first chapter not only prepares for the plot to follow but, also, for the themes as well. Silas' sterling moral parents give him a peaceful state of mind to which he returns; this brings the book to a happy ending, thus satisfying one requirement of *comedy*. His material fall owing to his moral flaw of greed in his dealings with Rogers is predicted to introduce an element of *tragedy*. Interweaving these two elements into one chapter displays Howells' ability to subtly present *tragicomedy*.

Silas' material rise is a *romantic* story, but it also sets the framework for a more *realistic* one dealing with his moral rise as a humanitarian who refuses to cheat the English settlers.

The Rise of Silas Lapham opens at the end of the protagonist's material rise and at the beginning of a moral one. It shows him to be a non-artistic man whose only claim to social position is money. These aspects are later discussed in these notes under the headings of morality, society, and art. The moral predicament that Silas is in is common to all Americans who can live profitably by exploiting others. These facets are considered under the heading Americanism and Universality.

CHAPTER II

Summary

Lapham returns to his home in the unfashionable South End section of Boston. The Laphams, who have come from the country, are unaware of the need of an acceptable location to help them gain social approval. They are not made aware of their poor location until Mrs. Corey calls on them to thank Mrs. Lapham for caring for her during an accidental meeting, when Mrs. Corey had become violently ill. She says that her driver had a difficult time finding the Lapham home. "Nearly all our friends are on the New Land or on the Hill," Mrs. Corey says.

Not only do the Laphams live in a socially unacceptable neighborhood, but also they have not educated their daughters to perform well in social functions; afraid of being snubbed by the other girls, the Lapham sisters dropped out of finishing school after attending part of a year.

When Mrs. Corey's son joins his mother at the Canadian water-
ing place where she has fallen ill, he impresses Mrs. Lapham with
his good manners. Persis sees a possible love affair between him
and Irene, but she realizes that her daughters have not been brought
up to match the Coreys socially.

The Laphams have spent their money on rich, ugly clothes,
costly, abominable frescoes, hotel rooms, and trips. They have
never thought of traveling to Europe, of giving dinner parties instead of treating an occasional businessman to potluck, or of building on their land in the better part of town.

"I declare," Mrs. Lapham says, "it [Mrs. Corey's aristocracy]
made me feel as if we had always lived in the backwoods."

Silas tells her he owns some property in the fashionable part
of town; he asks Persis if she wants to build on it. She says she does
not, but inwardly she is pleased and dreams of seeing her daughters
behind the windowpanes of a house on the New Land. Despite
Persis' protests, Silas decides to come out of the backwoods and
build on the land he owns, bringing his socially unacceptable
daughters out with him.

Commentary
This chapter substantiates the Laphams' lack of social or cul-
tural background. Silas feels that he can buy social position by
building a house in the right part of town. The house symbolizes the
culmination of his financial rise and, when it burns, a social goal he
cannot reach.

"The Laphams'," Howells tells us, "very strength of mutual
affection was a barrier to worldly knowledge; they dress for one
another; they equipped their house for their own satisfaction; they
lived richly to themselves, not because they were selfish, but because they did not know how to do otherwise." It is this lack of
concern for the rest of society that the Laphams must overcome
before they can morally take a place in society.

CHAPTER III

Summary
Irene receives a Texas newspaper containing an account of the Honorable Loring G. Stanton ranch. Her mother suspects that it is a love token from Tom Corey, who is spending the winter on a Texas ranch. Irene clips the account from the paper and saves it.

Lapham begins to build his house. His plan is the epitome of ugliness, and his architect is able to persuade him to make changes. When Silas visits the site with his wife, his old partner, Rogers, pays an unexpected call. Lapham will not speak to him and leaves the conversation which amounts to nothing, to Mrs. Lapham. Mrs. Lapham is reminded that the house is being constructed with part of a fortune amassed from capital Rogers originally put into Lapham's paint business. "I sha'n't live in it. There's blood on it," she says.

Persis firmly believes that Silas took advantage of Rogers by giving him the choice of either buying out or going out of the paint business. "You know he couldn't buy then. It was no choice at all. You unloaded [a partner] just at the time when you knew that your paint was going to be worth about twice what it ever had been; and you wanted all the advantage yourself. You crowded him out. A man that had saved you! No, you had got greedy, Silas. You had made your paint your god, and you couldn't bear to let anybody else share in its blessings."

Silas maintains that he never wanted a partner in the first place.

"If he hadn't put his money in when he did, you'd 'a' broken down," she retorts.

When Silas states that Rogers took more money out of the business than he put in, Persis reminds him that Rogers did not want to take his money out at all.

Commentary
The clipping is not from Tom Corey. It is later revealed that it is from a friend of Tom's; Tom thinks his friend might be interested

in Irene. This mistaken token of affection symbolizes the mistaken romance that is assumed by the romantic Laphams and Coreys.

Lapham's plan for an ugly home show his lack of aesthetic appreciation. He has marred the New England landscape with advertisement, and he will offend Bromfield Corey with his ignorance.

When Persis accuses Silas of taking advantage of Rogers and being a greedy man, who has made paint his god, she sets the purpose and the line of development for the rest of the novel. Howells purpose is to show modern businessmen that they must continue to live by the Golden Rule: "Do unto others as you would have them do unto you." Silas would not have wanted Rogers to force him out of a profitable paint business if the situation had been reversed; Lapham has morally wronged his neighbor. Howells shows how a modern businessman should act when Silas later refuses to extort money from English settlers to save his business. When Silas decides to treat his neighbor as he himself wants to be treated, his character changes, giving the novel the aspect of character development.

Howells does give Lapham's viewpoint on the matter, pointing out that Silas was influenced by his wife to acquire a partner and that Lapham let Rogers take more money out of the business than he put in. Mrs. Lapham argues effectively, however, saying that Silas needed a partner to maintain the business and that Rogers did not want to take his money out of the profitable paint business.

Which viewpoint Howells wishes his readers to take is debatable. Yet, it is difficult to believe that he desires his readers to see Silas Lapham as a man who did no wrong; this view would rid the book of the purpose for which Howells seemingly wrote it and would fail to emphasize any character development. It would indicate also that Howells condoned such business practices as Lapham used in forcing Rogers out of the paint business — a position known to be contrary to Howells' belief.

"Happy is the man for ever after who can choose the ideal, the unselfish part is such an exigency," Howells says in the next chapter. "Lapham could not rise to it."

CHAPTER IV

Summary

Persis Lapham is soon reconciled to the building of the new home, and they visit the construction again. This time they are visited by Tom Corey, who has just returned from Texas. Lapham takes a liking to him, although he later says that he doesn't approve of a young man living off his parents. "I like to see a man act like a man. I don't like to see him being taken care of like a young lady."

Commentary

Tom Corey's visit to the house brings him into the picture. He has returned from Texas, as Silas did, and eventually he will be part of the paint business. Silas' comment on the need for Tom to find something to do is a prediction of the position he will give him with the paint company.

CHAPTER V

Summary

Tom returns home to find his father, Bromfield Corey, home alone while his wife and daughters are at the seashore for the summer. They discuss Tom's desire to do something. Bromfield suggests marriage, but Tom does not regard it as an occupation. Bromfield goes on to suggest that Tom fall in love with a rich girl. Tom does not see how a poor girl would differ from a rich girl whose parents have not been wealthy long enough to give her position. Bromfield agrees that it is the age when the quickly rich are suddenly on the same level with the Coreys.

Howells relates that Bromfield was a painter who traveled to Rome, painted, and lived off his father. He made money only painting portraits, but, since he was wealthy, "It was absurd," Howells tells us, "for him to paint portraits for pay and ridiculous to paint them for nothing; so he did not paint them at all." Instead, Bromfield lived a life of seclusion, occasionally expounding on the theories of painting rather than practicing them.

The chapter ends with a few words between Mr. and Mrs. Lapham concerning Tom. "If I had that fellow in the business with me, I would make a man of him," Silas says.

"Do you suppose a fellow like young Corey, brought up the way he's been, would touch mineral paint with a ten-foot pole?" Mrs. Lapham jeers.

"Why not?" Silas haughtily replies.

Commentary
Tom's need for something to do, his father's avoidance of work, and Lapham's desire to make a man of Tom are clearly predictions of Tom's position with Lapham's business. His father has nothing to suggest, whereas Lapham has a prosperous business to offer.

Tom's comment that a rich girl would be no better than a poor girl if she did not have position is ironic, because, despite his ideal of marrying a socially acceptable rich girl, he marries Penelope, who is neither socially acceptable nor rich after her father's financial downfall.

CHAPTER VI

Summary
Tom Corey visits his mother at Bar Harbor to tell her that he is thinking of going into the Lapham paint business. Like her husband, Mrs. Corey objects to Lapham's defacing the countryside with his advertisements. "There was one of his hideous advertisements painted on a reef that we saw as we came down," she says.

Despite his mother's objections to this "common" man, Tom visits Lapham and offers to take over the selling of paint in foreign countries with his knowledge of French, German, and Spanish. He offers to sell on a commission, and Lapham decides to talk over the matter, taking Tom to his summer home.

During the boat trip, Lapham says he likes to rest his mind by reading his newspaper and looking at the people, whose faces always seem fresh to him.

Commentary

Mrs. Corey's objection to the Laphams on artistic and social grounds becomes even more important when Tom begins to court their daughter. Presently, however, the Coreys are only slightly perturbed because they realize that Tom's energy will lead him to involvement in some business enterprise. If only he had not chosen paint, they would be less repelled. Tom's vigor and ability to handle the job are displayed by his investigation of the Lapham business and his imaginative approach to staking out a position for himself in a foreign country.

Lapham's lack of refinement is shown by his commonplace expounding on the values of resting his mind. The people he enjoys and finds refreshing are really commonplace like himself and have only the poetry of vivid purpose to light them up, Howells comments.

CHAPTER VII

Summary

Lapham is bursting with pride when he tells his wife that Tom has come to him for a job. This completely contradicts her estimation of Tom the night before. Until now, Lapham had a definite dislike for the offensively aristocratic Coreys. He had treated the notion of Tom's affection for Irene with the contempt which such a ridiculous superstition deserved, Howells mentions. Yet, now as he watches the young people together, he is ready to accuse himself of being the inventor of a romance between the instantly liked Tom Corey and his beautiful daughter, Irene.

Commentary

Lapham's pride has nearly reached its peak, for he now has a Corey under his thumb. Also, his daughter may capture Tom as a husband, again raising their social position. Silas' greed has not been sated; he desires more social recognition. From this peak, he must fall and be humbled. He will be forced to face the reality of his crude background and the unjust way he made his money, his only claim to social position.

CHAPTER VIII

Summary
Mrs. Corey returns suddenly to check on Tom and is horrified that he has been taken into Silas' business. Bromfield says that he couldn't have been stopped; Tom would pay no heed to their opinions in this matter. Bromfield realizes that Tom is energetic but not brilliant; he does not think Tom would succeed in a profession, but he knows Tom wants to do something. Mineral paint is not much different from the other things Tom could go into, Bromfield feels.

Mrs. Corey objects more to the possibility of marriage between Tom and Irene than to Tom's going into the Lapham enterprise. She feels she could not get along with Irene, whom she says is insipid. "There is nothing to her," she states.

"The chief consolation that we American parents have in these matters is that we can do nothing," Bromfield consoles his wife. Parents no longer wholeheartedly interfere in marriage, he points out. "To which father in our acquaintance shall I go and propose an alliance for Tom with his daughter? I should feel like an ass," Bromfield observes.

Mrs. Corey resolves to speak to Tom about Irene when the time comes.

When Tom returns from his stay at the Laphams, Mrs. Corey tries to feel out any possibility of a love affair with Irene. She learns only that Tom's Uncle Jim has suggested the business venture, Penelope has a droll sense of humor, and Irene has a wonderful complexion. She reports to her husband that she has found out very little about the possibility of a romance between Tom and Irene. She states that she has found him with his mind made up concerning the business venture. She also realizes that there will be nothing she can do if Tom decides to marry Irene, but she hopes that he will not. Defeated, Mrs. Corey returns to the resort.

Tom has become engrossed in his work, and, upon returning to the office to pick up some work, he encounters a mysterious rendezvous between Silas and Zerrilla, a girl Lapham employs. Walker, the head bookkeeper, points out to Tom the next day that Lapham has always been secretive about the typist.

Commentary

This chapter recalls the Coreys' dislike for the Laphams, Tom's activeness in contrast with his father's passiveness, and the possibility of a romance between Tom and Irene. Even the Coreys are too romantic to ascertain that Tom, who talks mostly of Penelope, is attracted to her instead.

The mystery of Silas' connection with the typist is increased by Tom's encounter with her and by Walker's comments.

CHAPTER IX

Summary

This chapter delves further into Silas' social position. He does not treat Tom any better than one of his clerks; yet he likes to brag of Tom's presence on his staff. He believes that Tom is a born businessman and plots to have him marry Irene. Tom visits their new home and finds that, aside from business, horses, and the new house, he has little to talk about with Silas. He tries to suggest to Irene the books to include in their new library and gives her a wood shaving that they have amused themselves with.

He reports to his family that the Laphams do not read with any attention to quality, but that they are not unintelligent people. "They are very quick, and they are shrewd and sensible," he says.

"I have no doubt that some of the Sioux are so," his father retorts. "But that is not saying that they are civilized. All civilization comes through literature now, especially in our country." Bromfield, however, believes that there should be a dinner to recognize Tom's connection with the Laphams.

Silas is at the same moment wondering why there have been no such social overtures. He unrealistically maintains that his daughters are equal to Bromfields'. Irene is also wondering what can be done to further her romance. Penelope tells her that she doesn't have to do anything. "Whether this is either an advantage or a disadvantage, I'm not always sure," she says.

Commentary

Silas' pride is again indicated by his treatment of Tom as an underling and by his bragging of having a Corey employee. His thoughts of marrying Irene to Tom increase his pride, for he must convince himself that his daughters are equal to the Corey sisters.

Tom's suggestion of authors to be included in the Lapham's library is an instinctive action to help them become better citizens and more socially accepted. The wood shaving he gives to Irene is symbolic of the mistaken romance. Irene believes it to be a love token, but it is not. It is also from the new house, which is a larger symbol of romantic ideas.

The Coreys' conversation concerning civilization marks Lapham as being savage like the Sioux, which is a good comparison when his background is considered. "Civilization is not an affair of epochs and nations," Bromfield points out. "It's really an affair of individuals. One brother will be civilized and the other barbarian." In this conversation, Bromfield is hinting to Tom that Irene is not a girl of position, which is one of Tom's requirements in a wife.

Mrs. Lapham is aware that the Coreys are civilized and that they themselves are barbaric. Silas, however, contends that they are equal and should be invited to the Coreys' home or that they should even be able to make the first advances. "Oh, it isn't what you've got, and it isn't what you've done exactly. It's what you are," Mrs. Lapham tells Silas. "He's [Bromfield] been all his life in society, and he knows just what to say and what to do, and he can talk about the things that society people like to talk about, and you—can't. It puts him where he can make the advances without demeaning himself, and it puts you where you can't." She is for the moment being realistic about the situation.

Penelope's comment that Irene needs to do nothing to further her romance with Tom Corey is an expression of a romantic tradition which she questions. She predicts the rise of the aggressive modern woman.

CHAPTER X

Summary

Silas is spending too much on additions to the house, and Mrs. Lapham objects. She is greatly relieved when he reveals he has loaned the remaining money he planned to spend on the house to Rogers, who wishes to invest in some business venture.

Persis also objects to Silas' plot to match Tom Corey with Irene and has forbidden him to bring Tom home; however, Lapham uses her good mood over the Rogers loan to tax her patience and brings Corey home to dinner.

As Tom leaves after a talk with Penelope and Irene, he finds himself saying, "She's charming!" and laughing out loud.

Commentary

Lapham's loan to Rogers is the beginning of his financial downfall and his moral rise. His loaning the money that would have been put into the house is not accidental. He is investing in his moral salvation by drawing from his material welfare.

Corey's condition after talking with the Lapham girls indicates that he is enchanted with one of them. Howells is careful not to reveal which one, giving the reader an opportunity to be deceived by the Laphams' notion that he loves Irene. The reader does not definitely know of Tom's true feelings until the Laphams do.

CHAPTER XI

Summary

Tom, finding one of the Lapham girls quite charming, asks his father to visit Lapham. Bromfield decides to do it immediately the next morning.

Considering the Laphams move to the New Land, Bromfield asks Tom if the Laphams will be a great addition to society.

"No one can help feeling that they are all people of good sense and — right ideas," Tom replies.

"Oh, that won't do. Society is a very different sort of thing from good sense and right ideas. It is based upon them, of course, but the airy, graceful, winning superstructure which we all know demands different qualities. Have your friends got these qualities — which may be felt, but not defined?"

Tom must admit that the Laphams do not have these "felt" qualities.

When Bromfield visits Lapham's office, Silas' treatment of him is condescending, reducing Bromfield to the father of the boy to whom he generously gave employment.

At home that evening, Silas suggests inviting the Coreys to a housewarming, and his wife completely upbraids him for suggesting to take the first step. Their quarrel causes him sleeplessness, and he remains at home the next day. Tom Corey calls to see if Silas is well and is left alone in the parlor with Irene. He pays another visit later in the week and, again, is left alone with her. When he asks about Penelope, Irene persuades her sister to join them. Afterward Mrs. Lapham asks Penelope if Tom ever says anything about Irene. Penelope says that he has never mentioned Irene to her.

Confronting Silas with the problem, Persis says, "I can't make out whether he cares for her or not."

Commentary

Even now, when unknowingly Lapham is on the road to destruction, he is prideful to the point of insulting Bromfield Corey by his condescending attitude. His tragic fall is near, and, yet like other tragic figures, he is not aware of his fate until it happens. Only at the moment of his defeat will Lapham realize his tragic flaws of pride and greed.

Leaving Tom Corey and Irene alone advances the romantic love affair that has been built up in the minds of the Laphams. Still, Mrs. Lapham, who is somewhat perceptive, notes that Tom is not making the usual overtures about Irene.

CHAPTER XII

Summary

Mrs. Corey and her daughters, Nanny, a bookish girl, and Lilly, an artistic girl, return in the fall and begin to consider Tom's summer love affair. The possibility of having a sister-in-law or daughter-in-law who is repulsive is of the greatest irritation, because they know that once she is married to Tom, they will have to take her into their intimacy and show affection for her.

Bromfield maintains that Tom's visits are meaningless, but Mrs. Corey decides she must call on the Laphams; afterward she is still more repulsed by their nervousness during her call. Nevertheless, she decides they must have a dinner.

Commentary

The Corey women, despite their repulsion, submit themselves to the inevitability of having to recognize Tom's connection with the Laphams. They are Puritanical in their fatalistic view of life. They must submit, they feel, to what will happen even if they oppose it.

CHAPTER XIII

Summary

Mrs. Corey decides that a dinner including only close friends and relatives would be large enough to make the Laphams know that they are not ashamed of them and close enough to the Corey family to make the dinner insignificant to society. She tells Tom of the modest dinner party she has planned, and he realizes that his mother suspects the possibility of a romance deserving an appropriate dinner. He asks her not to give the party, but the invitations have been sent.

Mrs. Lapham worries about how she will answer the invitation, how she will dress, and, most important, how her family will find something to talk about. Silas decides he must buy his first dress coat and debates over the need for gloves. Penelope refuses to go, believing it is a recognition dinner for Irene. She cries after they leave, revealing her disappointment in her inability to be attractive like Irene. She also feels badly because, as it is later revealed, she is attracted to Tom.

Commentary

Ironically, this insignificant dinner will be one of the most crucial events in the novel. Its effect on Silas' social position will be seen in the next chapter. Mrs. Lapham predicts the impending disaster when she worries over what they will talk about. Penelope's absence and her sobs as they leave are significant, for the dinner will begin a chain of events that will lead to Tom Corey's declaration of love for her. Tom will see the Lapham's need for help in their social position; he will confess his love in order to aid the Laphams in finding a place in society.

CHAPTER XIV

Summary

The Laphams' arrival at the Coreys' house in an aristocratic, secluded neighborhood opens Chapter XIV. Silas' problems with gloves, which no one else wears, with the wine he drinks like the ice water served at his home table, and with the conversation he cannot follow and enter into are all brought out during the dinner party.

Bromfield Corey brings up the first topic of discussion—art. "You architects," he says to Mr. Seymour, Silas' architect, "and the musicians are the true and only artistic creators. All the rest of us, sculptors, painters, novelists, and tailors, deal with forms that we have before us; we try to imitate."

Bromfield instigates the next short discussion, also. He maintains that the rich ought to let the poor use their houses while they are absent during the summer.

"Surely, Bromfield," his wife says, "you don't consider what havoc such people would make with the furniture of a nice house!"

To this Bromfield weakly submits.

They continue by discussing the latest novel, *Tears, Idle Tears,* which is retitled "Slop, Silly Slop" by Nanny Corey. "There's such a dear old-fashioned hero and heroine in it, who keep dying for each other all the way through, and making the most wildly satisfactory and unnecessary sacrifices for each other. You feel as if you'd done them yourself," Miss Kingsbury says.

"Such old fashioned heroines are ruinous," Minister Sewell states. "The novelists might be the greatest possible help to us if they painted life as it is and human feelings in their true proportion."

When the men are alone, they talk of the need for more patriotic feelings among the young men. It is suggested that an occasion is needed. Bromfield Corey sees a need for good citizenship. "You can paint a man dying for his country, but you can't express on canvas a man fulfilling his duties as a good citizen," he points out.

"Perhaps the novelists will get him by and by," someone else suggests.

At this point Lapham finds occasion to enter the conversation and tells his war story. He speaks of Jim Millon's bravery in action when he saved Lapham by taking a bullet meant for him. Millon wanted to live for his wife Molly and his daughter Zerrilla, Lapham points out, but, like a real hero, he took an active part in the battle.

Silas has drunk too much wine, but he feels that now he has successfully talked and continues to tell Bromfield Corey about his paint. He continues drinking and expounding on different subjects until he has the talk altogether to himself; no one else talks, and he talks unceasingly.

Commentary
This chapter telling of the dinner party comes at the middle of the book, and like the first and last chapters, it is an important and

extensive one. It ties many threads of the story together and spins them out again; for instance, Silas' final social failure is a culmination of a quest, and it determines the falling action to follow as he retreats to the backwoods of his origins.

It predicts the situation in which Irene, Tom, and Penelope will soon be in by discussing the novel, *Tears, Idle Tears;* it is later revealed that the novel tells a story somewhat parallel to theirs. The discussion of the disproportion of this story is ironical, for it is happening before them and is caused by their own romantic notions.

Besides bringing the two families together and giving emphasis to what is to follow, Chapter XIV conveys many of Howells' ideas on art, society, and the romantic novel.

On art Howells says through the voices of Minister Sewell and Bromfield Corey, that most artists, like the novelists, are imitators. The best novelist, he says, will paint life as it really is and show human feelings in their true proportions. Howells, in writing a realistic novel that paints people as they really are, must show them as romantic characters, because many of the people of his time lived in an illusionary, romantic world. It is a world where they need the romantic flare of war to ignite them into good citizenship. Perhaps someday the novelist will show the nation that the man fulfilling his duties of a good citizen is just as exciting and rewarding as the soldier doing his duty by fighting with romantic valor in a war.

CHAPTER XV

Summary
In this brief chapter, Lapham apologizes to Tom Corey the day after the dinner party for his drunken behavior. Corey is more repulsed by his apology than by his behavior of the night before. After considering the Laphams' position, however, he decides that not only the Coreys but the Laphams could be hurt by the social fiasco, and he resolves to show them sympathy and respect.

Commentary
Silas is beginning to realize the reality of his social position. He says to Tom, "I was the only one that wasn't a gentleman there! I

disgraced you! I disgraced my family! I mortified your father before his friends!"

Tom's decision to help the Laphams is somewhat romantic and unrealistic, but it is a noble act that comes too late.

CHAPTER XVI

Summary

Tom is met by Penelope when he goes to Lapham's home to reveal his respect and sympathies. While waiting for Silas, they discuss the novel *Tears, Idle Tears,* which Penelope has recently read. "It's a famous book with the ladies," Tom says. "Did it make you cry?"

"Oh, it's pretty easy to cry over a book," says Penelope; "and that one is very natural till you come to the main point. Then the naturalness of all the rest makes that seem natural too; but I guess it's rather forced."

"Her giving him up to the other one?"

"Yes, simply because she happened to know that the other one had cared for him first. Why should she have done it? What right had she?"

"I don't know. I suppose that the self-sacrifice—"

"But it wasn't self-sacrifice—or not self-sacrifice alone. She was sacrificing him too; and for someone who couldn't appreciate him half as much as she could. I'm provoked with myself when I think how I cried over that book—for I did cry. It's silly—it's wicked for anyone to do what that girl did."

After pursuing other topics Tom declares his love for Penelope, much to her surprise. Penelope nearly slips and tells Tom that everyone had thought he was in love with Irene. She checks her words, however, but she pleads with Tom to leave and not to mention his feelings to her father.

Commentary

Although all the details of the novel *Tears, Idle Tears* are not given, a parallel between the romantic novel and the story of Penelope, Tom and Irene is somewhat evident. The hero in *Tears, Idle Tears* has not fallen in love with the girl who first cared for him. Likewise, Tom has fallen in love with Penelope rather than Irene. Penelope's attempt to give Tom up is also similar to the girl's self-sacrifice in *Tears, Idle Tears*. Penelope tells Tom, "You must go! And you must never come any more."

Her action is ironical, because she was provoked at the heroine's self-sacrifice in *Tears, Idle Tears*. "It's silly — it's wicked for anyone to do what that girl did," she had said. This incident helps to substantuate Howells' conviction that, in real life, people of his time often acted ridiculously romantic.

CHAPTER XVII

Summary

Penelope reveals the predicament to her mother the next day. Mrs. Lapham admits that Irene is not as mentally equal to Tom as Penelope, but she says she did not consider the possibility of Tom loving her older daughter. Although Penelope tried to avoid any personal contact with Tom, she admits that she tried to attract him.

Trying to find a solution to the problem, Penelope suggests the possibility of giving up Tom. "I've read of cases where a girl gives up the man that loves her so as to make the other girl happy that the man doesn't love. That might be done," she says.

"Your father would think you were a fool," retorts Mrs. Lapham.

Persis decides to confer with Silas before she reveals the situation to Irene. She sends a note to Silas, telling him to come home early that afternoon.

Commentary

The incapability of romantic women to face real problems is presented in this chapter. Neither Penelope nor her mother know how to handle the situation. Penelope avoids it by unloading it on her mother, while her mother turns to Silas for an answer.

CHAPTER XVIII

Summary

When Silas is told, he says that Penelope must marry Tom, if she wants him. Mrs. Lapham cannot see how this can be put into effect and believes that Silas wants to be related to the Coreys at the cost of Irene's feelings.

Silas seeks the advice of Minister Sewell. He supports Silas' opinion that Tom and Penelope should be married.

Commentary

After admitting his own lack of social grace, Lapham makes another realistic observation. He sees Penelope's self-sacrifice as being excessive and, therefore, romantic and unrealistic. Mrs. Lapham knows that Silas and Sewell are right, but she still finds it difficult to completely face the problem.

CHAPTER XIX

Summary

Mrs. Lapham forces herself to tell Irene of the situation. Stunned, the girl gives Penelope all her love mementoes: the newspaper clipping telling of the Texas ranch, the pine shaving, and a pin like one worn by one of Tom's sisters. She goes for a long walk with her father, buys a sleeping potion, and returns home to sleep. The next morning, she announces that she will go to the farming community of Lapham, named for Silas. Before she leaves, she instructs Penelope to tell Tom that they all thought he loved her.

Tom visits Penelope, who is still quite perplexed. He learns of the mistake and tries to convince Penelope that she must not be silly like the girl in the book, *Tears, Idle Tears*. However, she will not let him touch her, saying, "No, no! I can't let you — yet!"

Commentary

One critic has called this the greatest chapter in all literature. He praises the emotional impact of Irene's giving the love mementoes to Penelope. It is a sterling chapter, for it is one in which the symbols of romance are turned over to Penelope, and she must continue the romantic story. A good example of dramatic irony, it shows romance operating in reality, outside novels like *Tears, Idle Tears.*

The character of Irene is developed as she assumes the suffering which is rightfully hers. She must take it to spare the rest of the family. This illustrates Howells' concept of the "economy of pain" that must exist in a realistic world. Irene's decision to leave and her sleeping potion are both realistic solutions to her problem.

CHAPTER XX

Summary

Mrs. Lapham, who has accompanied Irene, returns from Lapham without her. Silas says that he will take the girl with him on a business trip to the West.

Lapham must try to sell mills Rogers has put up for collateral. He has lent Rogers too much money to protect the original loan and cannot pay his debts. "Pretty near everybody but the fellows that owe *me* seem to expect me to do a cash business, all of a sudden," he says.

He goes on to tell Persis that the mills Rogers has put up for collateral could have brought a good price until recently when a railroad took a ninety-nine-year lease on the only line going to them. If they decide to buy the mills, Rogers and Lapham would have to take the railroad's offer or carry the lumber and flour to market themselves.

Tom Corey, in the meantime, tells his mother the Lapham daughter he wishes to marry is not Irene but Penelope. Although surprised, Mrs. Corey instantly realizes the girl's awkward position,

but Bromfield Corey says, "Suppose the wrong sister had died —
would the right one have any scruples in marrying Tom? It's no
more shocking than reality. Why it's quite like a romance," he
concludes.

They both decide to bear up under the situation even though
Bromfield says, "When I talked to Silas, he poured mineral paint all
over me, 'till I could have been safely warranted not to crack or
scale in any climate."

Mrs. Corey points out that, at least, Penelope is not lacking
in sense. "She'll be quick to see that we don't mean unkindness.
The pretty one might have thought we were looking down on her,"
she says.

Commentary
Lapham's major task of trying to save his business has begun.
He has loaned Rogers too much money and now must depend upon
selling the mills at the price they were once worth.

The Coreys have no problem to solve but one to endure. They
must make the best of Tom's marriage. They accept their fate with
a certain amount of American submission which they have con-
sistently shown throughout the book.

CHAPTER XXI

Summary
Walker, Lapham's bookkeeper, senses financial problems and
mentions the situation to Tom Corey before Rogers appears. Lapham tells Rogers he has discovered that the mills Rogers put up
for collateral are almost worthless because of the strong hold the
G.L.&P. has on the railroad going to them. "I'm going to let the
mills go for what they'll fetch," Lapham says.

Rogers, however, has contacted some English agents who wish
to buy the mills. Not believing him, Silas gives him twenty-four
hours to produce the parties. "You bring me a party that will give
me enough for those mills to clear me of you, and I'll talk to you,"
Lapham says.

Yet, after considering the situation, Lapham begins to wrestle with his conscience over the morality of selling the property at a higher price than it is now worth. He spends the night thinking about it.

Commentary

Lapham's conscience is now beginning to work. He has recognized his place in society and knows that Penelope has been acting foolishly romantic. Now, taking another realistic look at the moral situation he finds himself in, he is troubled with the decision of whether to save his money or his soul. His realistic development prepares him for his moral choice and brings on his change in character.

CHAPTER XXII

Summary

Mrs. Lapham tells Penelope of her father's problems, and the girl immediately regains her composure and begins to think about something besides her problems with Tom Corey and Irene. She writes Tom a note and tells him not to visit her until she asks him. Silas enjoys a period of respite, as the English parties do not show up. During this impasse, to divert their minds, the family attends the theater. On another evening, Silas and Penelope work out business problems together to determine the actual state of affairs. Mrs. Lapham, who is actually better with the problems, is excluded because Silas does not wish her to know about all his business details. After Silas and Penelope finish, Mrs. Lapham finds a slip of paper listing payments made to a "Wm. M." Intending to give it to Silas later, she puts it into her sewing box but forgets it.

Commentary

Penelope's concern for her father helps her rise above her problems, as Silas does later by showing concern for the English settlers.

The diversion of the theater shows that this is a realistic situation in which there are moments of reprieve and escape.

CHAPTER XXIII

Summary
Lapham has nearly decided that he cannot sell the mills at an unfair price even if the English do make an offer. He stops work on the house and shuts down the paint works that have been operating twenty-four hours a day since he began. Heavy competition from an underselling West Virginia paint company and an overstocked market force Silas to admit his defeat.

After Silas tells Persis of these new developments, she remembers the slip of paper she has found and returns it to him. She asks who "Wm. M." is. Silas says it is nothing, tears the paper into small pieces, and drops them in the fire. The next morning, Mrs. Lapham finds a scrap of paper on the hearth with the name "Mrs. M." on it. Wondering what dealings her husband could have with a woman, and remembering his confusion about the paper, she asks him who "Mrs. M." is.

"I don't know what you're talking about," he answers.

"Don't you?" she returns. "When you do, you tell me." The matter is dropped.

At the office that day, Silas tells Tom Corey to get out of the business for his own good. Tom offers Lapham a loan, but Silas refuses.

After Lapham's conference with Corey, Zerrilla Dewey's mother invades his office to demand money to pay her rent and buy groceries. Lapham forces Mrs. Millon to leave but later gives Zerilla money. Zerrilla reveals the reason for the need of money; her husband, Dewey, returning from a sailing voyage, spent the night before drinking with her mother. Zerrilla tells Silas that she cannot divorce her husband, as she wishes, because he does not drink habitually or leave for longer than a year.

Lapham visits Zerrilla's home that evening to tell Dewey that he will support Mrs. Millon and Zerrilla, because Jim Millon took a bullet meant for him; but, he will not support anyone else, including Dewey.

Upon returning home, Silas tells Mrs. Lapham that he has lost money in the stock market in addition to his other financial problems. He mentions Tom Corey's offer of a loan, and Mrs. Lapham resolves to tell Penelope of Tom's offer.

In the meanwhile, Walker has indicated to Tom Corey that he believes there is something amiss in Lapham's relationship with Mrs. Dewey. Neither he nor Corey know the exact nature of the situation, but Walker says, "Accidents will happen in the best regulated families." He hints that Zerrilla might be Lapham's mistress, yet Corey is not willing to make such a quick assumption.

Commentary

Mrs. Lapham's discovery of the slip of paper with "Mrs. M." written on it lays the groundwork for her later suspicion that "Mrs. M." is Silas' typist. Because she believes it to be part of a payment slip, she later concludes, Howells hints, that the girl has been Silas' mistress.

Silas' visit to Mrs. Millon's home is realistically described and tends toward theatrical "naturalism," a kind of play that deals with the lower classes. Many critics found this repulsive in a day when romanticism, which upheld the noble and the beautiful, was still popular.

Tom shows his generosity and faith in Silas by offering him a loan. He has compassion and understanding that the rest of his society does not.

CHAPTER XXIV

Summary

Tom Corey investigates the seriousness of Lapham's financial problems and is told that, in addition to all other known problems, Lapham is competing with a company in West Virginia that can undersell him on a nearly stagnate market. While Corey is pondering the problem, he receives a thank you note from Penelope in gratitude for his financial offer. He wants to come to see her, but she will not let him.

Tom's uncle, Jim Bellingham, advises Silas to place himself in the hands of his debtors; but Silas' pride deters him, and he puts the house up for sale in an act of desperation. Silas cannot, however, part with this last concrete aspect of his life's work and social dreams and declines an offer to sell the next day. Going up to the house that night, he lights a fire in the chimney which, accidentally, burns down the house. The insurance had expired the week before, and Mrs. Lapham is relieved that no one can suspect Silas of burning it down purposely.

Commentary

Tom Corey's concern remains the most heartening element in the novel, but Silas and Penelope still have some justifiable pride; they refuse his offers of marriage and money. Lapham's pride, however, is still somewhat excessive, for instead of facing his brothers and the rest of the world as a bankrupt man, he puts his house into realtors' hands. The burning house symbolizes the destruction of Silas as a millionaire and the end of his social aspirations.

Penelope admits in this chapter that she has been excessively heroic. She reveals her reason for earlier sending a note to Tom Corey:

"I thought I ought to break with him at once, and not let him suppose that there was any hope for him or me if father was poor. It was my one chance, in this whole business, to do anything heroic, and I jumped at it. You mustn't think, because I can laugh at it now, that I wasn't in earnest, mother! I *was* — dead! But the Colonel has gone to ruin so gradually, that he's spoilt everything. I expected that he would be bankrupt the next day, and that then *he* would understand what I meant. But to have it drag along for a fortnight seems to take all the heroism out of it, and leave it as flat!"

CHAPTER XXV

Summary

Silas makes a last-ditch attempt to unite with the West Virginia paint company. They are friendly and willing to join with Silas if he can back them with enough capital to develop their enterprise. Silas cannot raise enough money, however, until Rogers presents the English agents, who offer Silas a sufficient sum for the mills even after he tells them of the situation; they are merely representatives for a group of wealthy English people and do not care how they spend the settlers' money.

Not giving the agents an answer, Silas returns home and finds Rogers there trying to convince Persis that the mills must be sold to save his family from poverty; if the mills are sold at the price the English offer, Rogers will be able to completely repay Silas and have enough money to take care of his family. Rogers has muddled Persis' mind to the point that she cannot help Silas make a decision when Rogers offers to buy the mills from Silas to relieve him of the responsibility of selling to the English.

Lapham paces the floor all night trying to decide what to do. Going to his office the next morning, he finds that the railroad's offer has come through. When Rogers arrives, he shows the letter to him, indicating that he will not sell to the English.

"You've ruined me!" Rogers cries. "I haven't a cent left in the world! God help my poor wife!"

This was Silas' reward for standing firm for right and justice to his own destruction; to feel like a thief and murderer, Howells comments.

Commentary

Silas has his most decisive battle with his conscience as he paces the floor all night trying to decide whether to sell to Rogers. As his wife listens to him walk the floor, this Biblical quotation comes to her mind: "And there wrestled a man with him until the breaking of the day. And he said, Let me go for the day breaketh.

And he said, I will not let thee go, except thou bless me." Silas wrestles with his conscience, which will not let go until he decides to make the right moral decision that indicates his self-sacrifice for others.

CHAPTER XXVI

Summary
        Lapham, on Bellingham's advice, goes to New York to ask the West Virginians for more time to raise the money. Mrs. Lapham, who feels remorse in not being able to help her husband make his decision in the English matter, attempts to visit him at his office for the first time in a year. She finds him gone and his typist in his office. When she returns home, she receives an anonymous note telling her to ask her husband who his typist is. This leads her to think Silas has been keeping a mistress; she has deduced that the girl could be "Mrs. M." — the name on the scrap of paper she found after Silas had torn the "Wm. M." payment slip apart. In a rage, she confronts him with this question when he returns. He does not answers her question and leaves for the town of Lapham without her knowing it.

Persis goes to his office only to discover that the typist is Zerrilla Millon Dewey, the daughter of the man who saved her husband's life. The misunderstanding resolved, she returns home to spend the day in self-reproach, wondering if Silas will ever return. Finally, she sends a note to Tom Corey to discover Silas' whereabouts. Irene returns, angry that they did not inform her of the trouble sooner; she starts to help by putting the household matters in order.

The next morning Tom tells his mother to visit the Laphams, indicating that he still intends to marry Penelope. The Coreys are caught in a trap. They have always said that they never cared for money. "And now we can't seem to care for the loss of it," Bromfield says. "That would be still worse."

Commentary

Mrs. Lapham as a romantic, unrealistic woman has completely failed her husband. She tries to be his conscience but could not help him decide whether or not to sell to the English. She would have let him sell and then plagued him with the need for repentance. This reaction is due to her romantic longings for wealth and her Puritan abhorrence for sin. She even fails to trust him in the case of Zerrilla and is shown to be foolish in her fears.

The Coreys are again shown as tolerant people who decide that they must pay the Lapham's a visit to acknowledge the love affair. They are fatalists and accept the worst.

CHAPTER XXVII

Summary

Silas returns from a conference with a man who wanted to unknowingly invest in the Lapham paint works; his money would have enabled Silas to close with the West Virginians. Silas cannot let him enter into the deal unaware and tells him the condition of his business. The offer is withdrawn, and Silas must put himself in his creditor's hands.

Lapham sells the South End home and moves back to the farm. The West Virginians confess they cannot produce a fine grade of paint like the Persis Brand; they let Silas handle this part of the enterprise after buying the mines and works at Lapham. This purchase relieves Lapham of the load of debt and gives him an interest in the vaster enterprise of the younger men.

Because of Silas' good standing with the West Virginians, Tom Corey goes with them. After marrying Penelope, he goes to Mexico to work in the foreign paint market.

Sewell, the pastor, interested in the moral spectacle which Lapham presented, visits him on the farm. When Sewell asks Lapham his conclusions on the moral question involving Rogers, Lapham replies, "It seems to me that I done wrong about Rogers in the first place. It was just like starting a row of bricks, I tried to catch and stop 'em from going, but they tumbled one after another." The English situation, Silas felt, was like a hole that opened for him, and he crept out.

Comment

Silas' morality does not fail him in his last temptation to let an unknowing New Yorker invest in his paint works. He returns to his backwoods origins as a final recognition that he finds dignity only in his pioneering traditions. He is a noble savage who does not belong in urban society.

Penelope's marriage does not advance him, for there is no longer any social contact with the Coreys. The Laphams are on the farm, the Coreys are in the city, and Penelope is in Mexico.

Silas' last words with the pastor show him to be aware of the reality of his moral fault. He knows that his act of self-sacrifice was the move that saved his soul, bringing his life to a happy ending after his tragic material downfall.

ANALYTICAL COMMENTARY

TRAGICOMEDY

The Rise of Silas Lapham is neither purely tragic nor purely comic; it is both. Tragicomedy is a form derived from drama which combines tragic and comic elements. Occasionally one scene will present the comedy and the next will present tragedy, but usually they are more subtly interwoven.

One view of tragedy calls for the downfall of a better than average man through some fault of his own. The destruction of Silas as a businessman accords well with this concept, for Silas, a wealthier than average man, loses his fortune owing to his greed. Silas' moral flaw is impressed upon his soul when he forces Rogers out of the paint business. His desire to buy redemption by giving Rogers a large loan that he cannot repay leads to Silas' destruction.

Comedy, also, places its character in a situation that he must resolve; but in comedy, the character overcomes the opposing forces, and the story ends happily. Seen as the rise of Silas' moral character, *The Rise of Silas Lapham* can be accepted as a comedy, for Silas redeems himself by refusing to save his business in a transaction that would transfer the mills at an unfair price to the English agents. Silas has overcome the oppressing force of materialism that has nearly damned his soul and finds peace of mind back on the farm where he was born.

The interweaving of the destruction of Silas as a businessman and his rise as a humanitarian categorizes *The Rise of Silas Lapham* as a tragicomedy. This view of the story leads to further appreciation of the integration of its romantic and realistic elements.

ROMANTICISM AND REALISM

William Dean Howells, an early advocator of realism, wrote novels that supported his beliefs. He included romantic elements in his novels, however, to show how they can be harmful in real situations. The rise of Silas from a barefoot farm boy to a millionaire is a romantic story which ends in financial disaster. Money and business are closer and more comprehensible than God to Silas, who needs a shower of cool moral realism.[2] Silas' moral rise fulfills Howells' desire to present an anti-romantic novel.

The secondary plot of the Irene-Penelope-Corey triangle love affair gives Howells another opportunity to defeat romantic ideas. The assumption that Tom loves Irene for her beauty rather than Penelope for her wit is a romantic notion held by both the Laphams and the Coreys. Howells shows us, of course, how unrealistic this notion is when Tom declares his love for Penelope. Additionally, he shows us how harmful it is to all the parties involved. Irene suffers humiliation, Penelope is placed in a frustrating position, and both the Laphams and the Coreys are forced to make major readjustments.

---

[2]Everett Carter, *The Age of Realism* (Philadelphia and New York: J. P. Lippincott Co., 1954), p. 235.

Penelope's desire to be heroic by giving up Tom is likewise romantic, for it shows her to be excessively self-sacrificing. She is not sparing her family from sorrow, like Irene, by re-establishing herself as a stronger person. As the minister Sewell points out in discussing the novel *Tears, Idle Tears,* "Old fashioned heroines are ruinous." Penelope's romantic and excessive sisterly love and self-sacrifice only make a realistic situation worse. She cannot realistically bring everything to a happy conclusion, as does the passive enduring, sweet coquette of the romantic novels.

Howells' realism extended beyond simply showing the ill effects of romantic notions. As a realist, he asked himself, "What can be known?" and turned to the average, commonplace lives of simple, individual human beings for an answer. He tried to look at each person in his novel with as much objectivity as possible, using realist dialogue and sensory images that would help the reader see the character more concretely. He knew the background of his characters and setting, and presented both good and bad aspects of each. His view of morality was realistic, seeing that the new world of business had to continue to base its morality on concern for other human beings. He wrote of men and women as they really were, often offending the romantic woman by teaching her to be more honest, more mature, more realistic, and healthier but usually making her lovable. In his stories, the male characters, who sorely need a woman capable of dealing with real problems, were also taught to be less greedy and more humanitarian.

Although his realism was not an infallible experiment to present the too-variable human nature factually, Howells did attempt to paint life as it is by presenting human feeling in true proportion, as Sewell recommends. He dealt with the commonplace — the aerial essence of life which, when interpreted, reveals the riddle of the painful earth, according to Bromfield Corey.

A note should be made indicating that Howells' realism is not altogether like that found in today's modern novels. For example, he avoids any sensual love scenes; his lovers seldom touch. Howells tells a story of people who fall in love, get married, have children, but never go to bed with one another.

Howells' ability to mix comedy and tragedy was, then, necessary when writing a realistic novel, which was in 1885 the most representative of this kind of writing. Establishing the concept of Howells' work as realistic is important, for it must also be considered as a realistic version of a morality play.[3] Silas is a modern-day Everyman, who, like the figure in medieval English church drama, must face temptation and overcome it.

MORALITY

Silas Lapham might be described as a "man who lived to himself without the knowledge of social good and evil."[4] A prideful materialist, Lapham must learn that he has to act without sole concern for himself. Living in a world where the code has become "every man for himself," Silas has to learn the moral need for self-sacrifice. His rise from self-centered egotism to concern for another, to concern for the group, to concern for society completes his destruction as a materialist. By refusing to unload his mills on the unsuspecting society of English settlers, he completes his moral rise and concludes his business failure.

Outward signs of Lapham's corruption are evident throughout the novel. His attempts to buy his social position with a costly house and his attempt to buy his way out of moral responsibility with a loan to Rogers are both comments on Lapham's low moral condition as well as a reflection upon the society in which he lives. Bromfield Corey recognizes the quandary of Silas' position, for it is caused by the society which Corey represents. His elegant but sterile society must make room for the progressive, rising businessman, but it can only admit these people on the basis of their material fortunes. Bromfield condemns his society for not helping morally isolated people like Silas with the struggle of good and evil. Lapham, uneducated and unrefined, must struggle with the temptation to maintain his social position by wealth or to lose it and return to his crude beginnings.

---

[3]Edwin H. Cady (ed.), *The Rise of Silas Lapham* (Riverside Editions; Boston, Mass.: Houghton Mifflin Co., 1957), p. v.
[4]Bennett, p. 162.

Lapham's moral rise and business failure, however, help him to make a social adjustment, even though it is a step back. Silas, at least, realizes that there are social differences between himself and the educated Coreys. Before his fall, he believes himself to be their equal, if not superior, in dollars. Later, he sees that without his money he is nothing, while the Coreys can survive socially without it.

His step back into the land of his origins re-establishes stronger roots for his family and gives them the dignity of a tradition not entirely based on quickly earned money. In his moral rise, Silas' pride is stiffled; he denies the temptation to seize every possible opportunity of trampling on others to gain material prosperity for himself. Bound again to his society, he learns to live for others. He outdoes even the Coreys as civilized man, for he triumphs over barbaric isolation. He learns to face the new set of values of the modern age by conforming to the old, basic rule of morality: Love Thy Neighbor. This humanitarian act of devotion is the only way to conceive of an all-loving God, bringing Lapham into contact with the spiritual world.

The moral rise of Silas Lapham, sparked with its elements of comedy and tragedy, told romantically and realistically, is made more pointed by Howells' use of symbols, which will be considered next.

SYMBOLISM

Houses
1. *The Back Bay Home* — The home built by Silas during his prosperity is the most far-ranging symbol of the book. It symbolizes the rise and fall of the materialistic Lapham himself. Just as Silas causes the house to burn by using the chimney one cold fall night, he also causes his own financial destruction by greed when he forces Rogers out of the business.

2. *The South End Home* — This is the home where much of the action of Lapham's story takes place. It represents Lapham's inability to rise socially as he rises materially. It is a home

of conflict, one that all are happy to leave because of the memories it holds in connection with Silas' downfall, the sisters' love affairs, and Mrs. Lapham's inability to help her husband in his moral decision.

3. *The Lapham Home* — This farm home symbolizes Lapham's native origins. Crude and in the backwoods, it takes its pride from the traditions of pioneering Americans.

4. *The Corey Home* — Symbolic of sterile aristocracy, the Corey home is described in detail when the Laphams come in contact with it for the dinner party. It represents the grace and elegance of the Coreys which will die because of their passive attitude toward the progressive, materialistic world. It will soon be in a neighborhood of boarding houses, Howells tells the reader.

The Wood Shaving

The wood shaving curled and given to Irene as a pseudo flower is analogous to the house symbol in the main plot. Irene must rise above the materialistic values that instigated the building of the Back Bay home and sacrifice her own feelings for the good of the families. She gives the shaving to Penelope when she realizes that Tom Corey did not mean it to be a love token for her. In giving it to Penelope, she relinquishes her part in a romantic, materialistic world.

After considering the morality needed by Silas and his family with reference to the symbols which help to convey their moral position, it is necessary to look at the society that caused this moral dilemma.

SOCIETY

The problem of a sudden material rise placing a man in a responsible position socially is considered by Howells in *The Rise of Silas Lapham*. What can Silas Lapham do for civilization besides cover its countryside with advertisements for his paint? Obviously nothing. When Bromfield Corey points out that civilization is really an affair of individuals rather than epochs and nations, he is pointing a finger at Lapham. He clarifies himself further by saying, "One brother will be civilized and the other barbarian."

Silas, whose main pursuits outside of business are the newspaper, theater, and lectures, does not fulfill Bromfield's description of a civilized man. "All civilization comes through literature," Bromfield states, and Lapham is not a reading man. Commenting on drama in his time, Corey says, "Theater is intellectually degrading," and newspapers and lectures are not to him complete sources of civilized thought.

The Laphams seldom buy books and believe too much reading is harmful to health. Most of the books brought into the house are borrowed from the library. When Irene discusses with Tom Corey stocking the library of their new home with books, she finds herself on unsure ground; she suggests buying Gibbon's works.

"If you want to read him," Corey replies. "You'll want Green, of course, and Motley and Parkman."

"Yes," she answers. "What kind of writers are they?"

"They're historians too."

"Oh yes; I remember now. That's what Gibbon was. Is it Gibbon or Gibbons?"

What is society doing to help the newly rich become well-read, civilized people? The answer is again, nothing. The conventional, closed, Bostonian society finds it impossible to entertain people like the Laphams just as they cannot let the poor use their homes while they are gone in the summer for fear that they will break the furniture. The Laphams might well break some of the out-dated ideas of this obsolete culture which suffers from romantic pride.

Silas and other businessmen like him demand a creative solution to a problem the Bostonian elite were unable to face. Only Tom attempts to help the Laphams choose the best authors for their library and, by marrying Penelope, takes the responsibility of raising her to his level. "The children can learn their ways," Mrs. Lapham says.

Society, however, cannot accept Silas or find a way to make him acceptable. An airy, graceful, winning superstructure is something Silas cannot buy. He has right ideas and good sense; but these are only fundamentals, and society demands additional superficialities. The social dilemma caused by the rise of uncouth men of wealth also involves the artist, such as Bromfield Corey. Therefore, art is the next topic that will be briefly considered.

ART

What happens to art when men like Silas Lapham come into power? The result could have been ludicrously illustrated if Lapham had been allowed to build the home of his dreams. Without the guiding hand of Seymour, the Lapham home would have been the epitome of ugliness. Lapham, who can afford to be artistic, has none of the aesthetic inklings that are necessary. The domination of art by a blundering capitalist can be disastrous, Howells points out, especially if our artists are as weak as Bromfield Corey.

Elegant but sterile in his art, Corey can talk about it, but he cannot effectively practice it. He retreats into a world of seclusion and theories, never becoming actively engaged in producing an object of outstanding art. The largeness of Silas' project reflects his activity and drive, but Lapham's conception of it could have been harmful to the artistic world. If artists are not active, art is in great danger, Howells is saying.

Lapham's moral rise from self-concern to concern for society is not accidental, for we must not view *The Rise of Silas Lapham* as merely a story of one inartistic man or of Bostonian society. Its message is far-reaching with a universality that touches the entirety of American society even today.

AMERICANISM AND UNIVERSALITY

In writing a realistic novel, Howells shows us a true picture of the American—good and evil, benevolent and prideful, foolish and wise, strong and weak. His story has a message to all American men who are still tempted by the pressure of their way of life to lie, cheat, steal, bluff, maneuver, conceal, and evade—men who still desire to exalt themselves by crushing others for money, power, and prestige, instead of living for the good of others.

Also American women can learn from Howells' parable until they are free from the fantasies of emotional agony, heroically surmounted by overwhelming self-sacrifice.[5] When Americans take a more realistic look at life and live by it, Howells' story will be outdated.

QUESTIONS AND ANSWERS

PLOT

Is the plot probable?

Although the plot of *The Rise of Silas Lapham* often seems somewhat contrived, it is probable; men have made and lost fortunes; other men have fallen in love with one girl, while being supposedly in love with another. Less likely is the return of Rogers at the moment Silas tries to climb the social ladder. When Rogers produces English agents willing to buy the mills at a high price, the story again seems a bit contrived. Yet, even these incidents could occur. They are surprises which sometimes happen.

Is the plot employed to convey ideas?

If Howells does employ facts in his plot that are not completely probable, he does it to convey ideas. His illustration of businessman's need for integrity based on sound moral judgment is shown through the events of Silas Lapham's life. Howells' plot is additionally used to express his ideas on art, the novel, and society. Quite

---

[5]Cady, p. xviii.

often he simply has one of his characters, usually Bromfield or Sewell, make a statement on one of these ideas. Most of the time their statements are related to the plot; only occasionally Howells has them speak merely for the sake of discussion.

Is the plot simple or complex?

Two stories are told in *The Rise of Silas Lapham:* (1) Silas' financial rise and fall and (2) Penelope's, Tom's and Irene's love story. The presence of two stories makes the plot only somewhat complex.

Are the two stories united? Silas' determination to be both wealthy and socially accepted is the strongest element in bringing the two stories together. He wants his daughter to marry into the aristocratic Corey family to enhance his position in society. Silas' life is guided by the words "I want." His greed also causes him to gain and lose a fortune. By forcing Rogers out of the paint business, he increases his wealth. Yet, because he is greedy, he invests too much in the stock market and fails. Remembrance of his slight to Rogers also causes him to lose money when he makes Rogers a loan. Both plots, then, are strongly related to Lapham's desire "to have," and this compulsion brings the two stories together.

Does the plot revolve around a conflict?

The most important conflict in *The Rise of Silas Lapham* is Silas' battle with his conscience. Did he wrong Rogers when he forced him out of the business? Can he rightfully sell the mills to the English for more than they are worth? When Silas spends the night trying to come to a decision on the mills, his wife is reminded of the Bibical character Jacob wrestling with an angel. When this conflict is resolved by Silas' decision not to sell to the English, the climax is reached, and the falling action of the novel begins.

TECHNIQUE AND STYLE

Is the novel presented dramatically or through summarized narration?

Howells employs both dramatic scenes and summarized narration. This might be exemplified by the first chapter of *The Rise of*

Silas Lapham. Howells presents the interview between Bartley Hubbard and Lapham during which Lapham's past life is dramatically told in the interview and summarized by interspersing parts of Hubbard's report.

Does Howells employ humor?

Penelope, Bromfield, and Hubbard can be counted upon to give humorous accounts in many of the book's situations. Through them Howells brings humor to the novel. Penelope, for example, tells Tom that upon meeting his father for the first time after her engagement "he was sitting with his hat on his knees, a little tilted away from the Emancipation group, as if he expected the Lincoln to hit him."

When Bromfield refers to the occasion, he says, "Fancy Tom being married in front of the group, with a floral horse-shoe in tuberoses coming down on either side of it!"

In the first chapter, Bartley Hubbard is also used for comic relief. After Lapham names the various uses for his paint, Hubbard says, "Never tried it on the human conscience, I suppose."

Does Howells employ satire?

Satire, which is usually humor pointed at society, occasionally occurs in Howells' novel. In Chapter X, for example, the author says:

A man has not reached the age of twenty-six in any community where he was born and reared without having had his capacity pretty well ascertained; and in Boston the analysis is conducted with an unsparing thoroughness which may fitly impress the un-Bostonian mind, darkened by the popular superstition that the Bostonians blindly admire one another.

What artistic skills are apparent in Howells' dialogue?

To gain realism Howells attempts to fit his dialogue to his characters. Silas often says "aint't" and "hain't," whereas Bromfield Corey seldom makes a grammatical error. Conversations presented in this novel usually consist of short speeches which aid Howells in achieving a naturalistic effect.

What is one of Howells' special devices?

One of Howells' special devices is to leave some major aspects of his novel to the readers' conclusions. For instance, Howells never sets down an ultimate judgment on the morality of Laphams' maneuver to force Rogers out of the paint business. Persis claims, in the last part of the third chapter, that Silas has taken advantage of Rogers when he gave Rogers the choice of buying out or going out of the paint business. "You know he couldn't buy out then. It was no choice at all," she reminds him. "You unloaded [a partner] just at the time when you knew that your paint was going to be worth about twice what it ever had been; and you wanted all the advantage for yourself."

Silas maintains that he did not want a partner in the first place. "If he hadn't put his money in when he did, you'd 'a' broken down," Persis argues effectively.

"Well, he got his money out and more, too," Silas wearily defends himself.

"He didn't want to take it out," Persis answers.

In the next chapter, Howells casts a doubt over Silas' guilt so effectively maintained by Persis argument. Howells states:

As he said, Lapham had dealt fairly by his partner in money; he had let Rogers take more money out of the business than he put into it; he had, as he said, simply forced out of it a timid and inefficient participant in advantages which he had created. But Lapham had not created them all. He had been dependent at one time on his partner's capital. It was a moment of terrible trial. Happy is the man for ever after who can choose the ideal, the unselfish part in such an exigency! Lapham could not rise to it.

Whether Silas was guilty or not is never determined; Howells leaves this quandary open to opinions. He uses Silas' feeling of guilt about the matter, however, to determine the character change of this central character. Silas tries to make up the slight to Rogers by loaning him money.

This loan and numerous other factors make payment of debts impossible for Silas. His only hope is to transfer the mills Roger has put up for collateral to English settlers at a price which is more than the mills are worth. Recalling his possible injustice to Rogers, Silas considers the morality of selling the mills at an unfair price. He decides to free himself of any possible moral guilt and refuses to complete the transaction. Silas' character changes at this point, for he admits the possibility of guilt in forcing Rogers out of the business and will not multiply his guilt in a business deal that would harm others. Lapham says in the concluding chapter:

> "It seems to me I done wrong about Rogers in the first place; that the whole trouble came from that. It was just like starting a row of bricks. I tried to catch up and stop 'em from going, but they all tumbled, one after another. It wan't in the nature of things that they could be stopped till the last brick went.... Seems sometimes as if it [the English incident] was a hole opened up for me, and I crept out of it."

Although Howells leaves this question of morality open, he effectively shows that a modern businessman must still be aware of the saying, "Do unto others as you would have them do unto you." Howells himself advocated a moral outlook on business ventures, but he left it to his readers to decide whether a strong sense of moral justice must be maintained in business matters.

The author leaves other more minor points to the reader's perception. He never tells whether Lapham accepted the railroad's offer. Silas does show the railroad's letter, offering to buy the mills to Rogers as an indication of his refusal to sell to the English. Yet, Howells never definitely says Lapham sold to the railroad. Neither does Howells give any indication that Lapham did otherwise.

One mystery Howells never reveals is the authorship of the note to Mrs. Lapham. The note simply says, "Ask your husband about his lady copying-clerk [typist]. A Friend and Well-wisher."

When Persis shows the note to Silas, he says, "I guess I know who it's from, and I guess you do, too Persis."

"But how—how could he—," she replies.

"Mebbe he believed it," Silas answers. "You did."

Walker, Lapham's bookkeeper had been the one who hinted the most of an illicit relationship between Silas and Mrs. Dewey. Still, the note is signed "A Friend and Well-wisher." Also, Mrs. Lapham says, "But how—how could he—." These facts might point more to Tom Corey than to Walker. Whoever sent the note is not named, however; again Howells lets the reader decide.

QUESTIONS

1. What is the relationship of the business story to the love story? (Introduction and Plot Summary)

2. Is Silas Lapham a tragic or comic character? (Silas)

3. What is Persis Lapham's moral outlook on life? (Persis)

4. Why is Penelope a romantic heroine? (Penelope)

5. What is Bromfield Corey's view of civilization? (Bromfield)

6. What is Tom Corey's function in the book in regard to society? (Tom)

7. Why is this novel a tragicomedy? (Tragicomedy)

8. What is Howells' view of romanticism as opposed to realism? (Romanticism and Realism)

9. What constitutes Silas' moral rise? (Morality)

10. What is the condition of the late 1800 American society? (Society)

11. Is Bromfield Corey a true artist? (Art)

12. What has happened to art with the rise of the middle class? (Art)

13. What message does *The Rise of Silas Lapham* have for Americans today? (Americanism and Universality)

14. What is the significance of Lapham's statement on his advertisements? (Chapter I)

15. Who makes the Laphams aware of their unfashionable neighborhood? (Chapter II)

16. How does Mrs. Lapham feel about Silas' relationship with his former partner? (Chapter III)

17. What is Silas' reaction when he first encounters Tom Corey? (Chapter IV)

18. Give the background of Bromfield Corey's life. (Chapter V)

19. How does Tom Corey propose to join the Lapham paint business? (Chapter VI)

20. Why does Silas' attitude change toward the Coreys? (Chapter VII)

21. What does Bromfield Corey say about American parents? (Chapter VIII)

22. How does Lapham treat Tom Corey during office hours? (Chapter IX)

23. What does Lapham do with some of the money he had planned to spend on his new home? (Chapter X)

24. Does Bromfield consider the Laphams fit for society? (Chapter XI)

25. How do the Corey girls feel about Irene? (Chapter XII)

26. What does Mrs. Lapham worry about during her preparations for the Corey's dinner party? (Chapter XIII)

27. What does Bromfield Corey say about art? (Chapter XIV)

28. What is the significance of Lapham's apology for his drunken behavior? (Chapter XV)

29. What is Penelope's reaction when Tom Corey declares his love for her? (Chapter XVI)

30. What does Penelope suggest she do in the situation in which Tom Corey has placed her? (Chapter XVII)

31. How does Sewell propose to solve Penelope's problem? (Chapter XVIII)

32. What does Irene do when she knows Tom does not love her? (Chapter XIX)

33. What happens to the mills Rogers put up for collateral? (Chapter XX)

34. What unusual offer does Rogers make concerning the mills? (Chapter XXI)

35. What is written on the slip of paper Mrs. Lapham finds? (Chapter XXII)

36. What does Silas have to do when he discovers the weight of his financial problem? (Chapter XXIII)

37. How does Silas burn his new home down? (Chapter XXIV)

38. What does Rogers propose that Lapham do to ease his conscience in the English matter? (Chapter XXV)

39. With whom does Silas try to unite his business? (Chapter XXVI)

40. What does Silas say about his relationship with Rogers? (Chapter XXVII)

THEME TOPICS

1. Compare and contrast Silas Lapham to Bromfield Corey.

2. Show how realism combats and defeats romanticism in this novel.

3. Compare Howells to Mark Twain or Henry James.

4. Show how *The Rise of Silas Lapham* could be looked at as a social satire or a comedy of manners.

5. Show how *The Rise of Silas Lapham* portrays the death of Puritanism.

6. Show how Silas' self-sacrifice is different from Penelope's self-sacrifice.

BIBLIOGRAPHY

Bennett, George N. *William Dean Howells: The Development of a Novelist.* 1959.

Carter, Everett. *The Age of Realism.* 1954.

Cady, Edwin H., ed. *The Rise of Silas Lapham.* 1957.

Jeffrey, H. R. *The Realism of William Dean Howells.* 1921.

Harvey, Alexander. *A Study of the Achievement of a Literary Artist.* 1917.

Howells, William Dean. *Criticism and Fiction.* 1891.

NOTES

NOTES